Early Masonic Symbolism

By Manly P. Hall

Copyright © 2022 Lamp of Trismegistus. All rights reserved. No part of this publication may be reproduced or transmitted in any form or by any means, electronic or mechanical, including photocopying, recording, or by any information storage and retrieval system, without permission in writing from Lamp of Trismegistus. Reviewers may quote brief passages.

ISBN: 978-1-63118-606-6

*Foundations of Freemasonry
Series*

Other Books in this Series and Related Titles

Masonic and Rosicrucian History by M P Hall & H Voorhis (978-1-63118-486-4)

The Kabbalah of Masonry & Related Writings by E Levi &c (978-1-63118-453-6)

Some Deeper Aspects of Masonic Symbolism by A E Waite (978-1-63118-461-1)

Masonic Symbolism of King Solomon's Temple by A Mackey &c (978-1-63118-442-0)

The Old Past Master by Carl H Claudy (978-1-63118-464-2)

The Influence of Pythagoras on Freemasonry and Other Essays (978-1-63118-404-8)

The Mysteries of Freemasonry & the Druids by various (978-1-63118-444-4)

Rosicrucians and Speculative Masonry in the Seventeenth Century (978-1-63118-489-5)

The Two Great Pillars of Boaz and Jachin by A Mackey &c (978-1-63118-433-8)

The Regius Poem or Halliwell Manuscript by King Solomon (978-1-63118-447-5)

The Lost Keys of Freemasonry or The Secret of Hiram Abiff (978-1-63118-427-7)

The Master Mason's Handbook by J S M Ward (978-1-63118-474-1)

Brothers & Builders by Joseph Fort Newton (978-1-63118-506-9)

Symbolism and Discourses on the Entered Apprentice, Fellowcraft and Master Mason Blue Lodge Degrees by various (978-1-63118-413-0)

Freemasonry in the Medieval or Middle Ages by various (978-1-63118-450-5)

American Indian Freemasonry by A C Parker (978-1-63118-460-4)

Freemasonry, Mithraism and the Ancient Mysteries by various (978-1-63118-407-9)

The Ceremony of Initiation: Analysis & Commentary (978-1-63118-473-4)

The Symbols and Legends of Masonry by C H Vail (978-1-63118-504-5)

The Janeites, The Man Who Would Be King and Other Stories of Freemasonry by Rudyard Kipling (978-1-63118-480-2)

Audio Versions are also available on Audible, Amazon and Apple

Other Books in this Series and Related Titles

Rosicrucian Rules, Secret Signs, Codes and Symbols by various (978-1-63118-488-8)

History and Teachings of the Rosicrucians by W W Westcott &c (978-1-63118-487-1)

The Rosicrucian Chemical Marriage by Christian Rosenkreuz (978-1-63118-458-1)

The Rosicrucian Fama Fraternitatis and Confessio Fraternitatis (978-1-63118-454-3)

Freemasonry and the Egyptian Mysteries by C. W. Leadbeater (978-1-63118-456-7)

Qabbalistic Teachings and the Tree of Life by M P Hall (978-1-63118-482-6)

The Sepher Yetzirah and the Qabalah by M P Hall (978-1-63118-481-9)

The Comte de St. Germain: The Secret of Kings (978-1-63118-525-0)

The Eleusinian Mysteries and Rites by Dudley Wright (978-1-63118-530-4)

The Psalms of Solomon by King Solomon (978-1-63118-439-0)

The Legend of the Holy Grail and its Connection with Templars and Freemasons by A E Waite (978-1-63118-462-8)

Masonic Symbolism of the Apron & the Altar by various (978-1-63118-428-4)

The Book of Wisdom of Solomon by King Solomon (978-1-63118-502-1)

Masonic Symbolism of Easter and the Christ in Masonry (978-1-63118-434-5)

The Odes of Solomon by King Solomon (978-1-63118-503-8)

Ancient Mysteries and Secret Societies by M P Hall (978-1-63118-410-9)

The Golden Verses of Pythagoras: Five Translations (978-1-63118-479-6)

Freemasonry & Catholicism by Max Heindel (978-1-63118-508-3)

A Few Masonic Sermons by A. C. Ward &c (978-1-63118-435-2)

The A. E. Waite Reader: A Selection of Occult Essays (978–1–63118–515–1)

The Leadbeater Reader: A Selection of Occult Essays (978-1-63118-483-3)

Audio versions are also available on Audible, Amazon and Apple

Table of Contents

Series Introduction...7

Early Masonic Symbolism

Part I: *Origins in Biblical Fables*...9

Part II: *The Dionysiac Architects*...15

Part III: *Solomon, the Personification of Universal Wisdom*...23

Part IV: *Freemasonry's Priceless Heritage*...31

INTRODUCTION

From the beginning of Modern Freemasonry's birthdate of 1717, the intelligentsia of humanity have found refuge for safe reflection within the walls of the fraternity. Masonic writers have produced a nearly incalculable amount of written musings on a multitude of esoteric and philosophical subjects, as they relate to the ancient mysteries that Freemasonry currently storehouses. Sadly, most of it appears to have sat largely unread, as American Freemasonry in particular, continues to transform itself into something that bears little resemblance to what it was originally designed to be. The true essence of Freemasonry is not that of blind patriotism or a single-minded national religion but one of Universal Brotherhood and altruism, designed for the betterment not just of its members but of society as a whole. In particular, for those who are not members of the fraternity, as Freemasonry has always acted as a beacon, to help guide humanity through darker times, with the hopes that one day we will collectively reach a truly enlightened age.

It's not uncommon for new members joining the fraternity to find little education within the walls of many modern lodges, in spite of so much written material available to the membership. Many older members are not simply uneducated with regards to real Masonic history and symbology, not to mention the vast arena of related subjects, but they are disinterested in all of it, as well.

Lamp of Trismegistus is doing its part to help preserve humanity's Masonic history by making some of these classics available to those students who are seeking to unearth the knowledge of these ancient colossi. As such, Lamp of Trismegistus offers its readers highlights of Masonic study, culled from a variety of authors and viewpoints, with the hope bringing education back into the fraternity. So, be sure to check out other titles in our *Foundations of Freemasonry Series* as well as our *Theosophical Classics, Occult Fiction, Paranormal Research Series, Esoteric Classics, Supernatural Fiction, Studies in Buddhism* and our *Christian Apocrypha Series* as well as numerous other subjects; and, don't be afraid to let a little altruism into your own heart or even into your Lodge. You can also download the audio versions of many of these titles from Audible, Amazon or Apple, for learning on the go.

EARLY MASONIC SYMBOLISM

PART I:

Origins in Biblical Fables

In several early Masonic manuscripts--for example, the Harleian, Sloane, Lansdowne, and Edinburgh-Kilwinning--it is stated that the craft of initiated builders existed before the Deluge, and that its members were employed in the building of the Tower of Babel. A Masonic Constitution dated 1701 gives the following naive account of the origin of the sciences, arts, and crafts from which the major part of Masonic symbolism is derived:

"How this worthy Science was first begun, I shall tell. Before Noah's Flood, there was a man called Lameck as it is written in the 4th Chapter of Genesis: and this Lameck had two Wives. The one was called Adah, and the other Zillah; by the first wife Adah he got two Sons, the one called Jaball, and the other Juball, and by the other wife Zillah he got a Son and Daughter, and the four children found the beginning of all Crafts in the world. This Jaball was the elder Son, and he found the Craft of Geometric, and he parted flocks, as of Sheep and Lambs in the fields, and first wrought Houses of Stone and Tree, as it is noted in the Chapter, aforesaid, and his Brother Juball found the craft of Music, of Songs, Organs and Harp. The Third Brother [Tubal-cain] found out Smith's craft to work Iron and Steel, and their sister Naamah found out the art of Weaving. These children did know that God would take Vengeance for Sin, either by fire or water, where for they wrote these Sciences which they had found in Two Pillars of stone, that they might be found after the Flood. The one stone was called Marble—it can not burn with Fire, and the other was called Laturus [brass], it can not drown in the Water." The author of this Constitution there upon declares that one of these pillars was later discovered by Hermes, who communicated to mankind the secrets thereon inscribed.

In his *Antiquities of the Jews,* Josephus writes that Adam had forewarned his descendants that sinful humanity would be destroyed by a deluge. In order to preserve their science and philosophy, the children of Seth therefore raised two pillars, one of brick and the other of stone, on which were inscribed the keys to their knowledge. The Patriarch Enoch--whose name means the Initiator--is evidently a personification of the sun, since he lived 365 years. He also constructed an underground temple consisting of nine vaults, one beneath the other, placing in the deepest vault a triangular tablet of gold bearing upon it the absolute and ineffable Name of Deity. According to some accounts, Enoch made two golden *deltas*. The larger he placed upon the white cubical altar in the lowest vault and the smaller he gave into the keeping of his son, Methuseleh, who did the actual construction work of the brick chambers according to the pattern revealed to his father by the Most High. In the form and arrangement of these vaults Enoch epitomized the nine spheres of the ancient Mysteries and the nine sacred strata of the earth through which the initiate must pass to reach the flaming Spirit dwelling in its central core.

According to Freemasonic symbolism, Enoch, fearing that all knowledge of the sacred Mysteries would be lost at the time of the Deluge, erected the two columns mentioned in the quotation. Upon the metal column in appropriate allegorical symbols he engraved the secret teaching and upon the marble column placed an inscription stating that a short distance away a priceless treasure would be discovered in a subterranean vault. After having thus faithfully completed his labors, Enoch was translated from the brow

Of Mount Moriah. In time the location of the secret vaults was lost, but after the lapse of ages there came another builder--an initiate after the order of Enoch--and he, while laying the foundations for another temple to the Great Architect of the Universe, discovered the long-lost vaults and the secrets contained within.

John Leylande was appointed by King Henry VIII to go through the archives of the various religious institutions dissolved by the king and remove for preservation any books or manuscripts of an important character. Among the documents copied by Leylande was a series of questions and answers concerning the mystery of Masonry written by King Henry VI. In answer to the question, "How came Masonry into England?" the document States that Peter Gower, a Grecian, traveled for knowledge in Egypt, Syria, and every land where the Phœnicians had planted Masonry; winning entrance in all lodges of Masons, he learned much, and returning, dwelt in Greater Greece. He became renowned for his wisdom, formed a great lodge at Groton, and made many Masons, some of whom journeyed in France, spreading Masonry there; from France in the course of time the order passed into England.

To even the superficial student of the subject it must be evident that the name of *Peter Gower*, the Grecian, is merely an Anglicized form of *Pythagoras;* consequently Groton, where he formed his lodge, is easily identified with Crotona. A link is thus established between the philosophic Mysteries of Greece and mediæval Freemasonry. In his notes on King Henry's questions and answers, William Preston enlarges upon the vow of secrecy as it was practiced by the ancient initiates. On the authority of Pliny he describes how Anaxarchus, having been imprisoned in order to extort from him some of the secrets with which he had been entrusted, bit out his own tongue and threw it in the face of Nicocreon, the tyrant of Cyprus. Preston adds that the Athenians revered a brazen statue that was represented without a tongue to denote the sanctity with which they regarded their oath-bound secrets. It is also noteworthy that, according to King Henry's manuscript, Masonry had its origin in the East and was the carrier of the arts and sciences of civilization to the primitive humanity of the western nations.

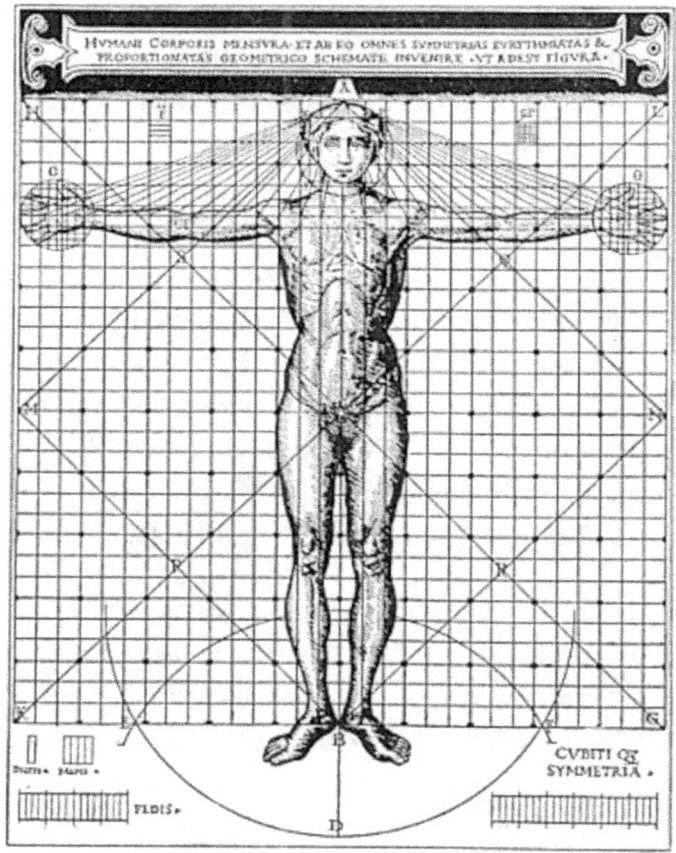

THE MYSTERY OF THE MACROCOSM[1]

---

[1] Redrawn from *Cesariano's Edition of Vitruvius*.

Summarizing the relationship between the human body and the theory of architectonics, Vitruvius writes:

"Since nature has designed the human body so that its members are duly proportioned to the frame as a whole, it appears that the ancients had good

Conspicuous among the symbols of Freemasonry are the seven liberal arts and sciences. By *grammar* man is taught to express in noble and adequate language his innermost thoughts and ideals; by *rhetoric* he is enabled to conceal his ideals under the protecting cover of ambiguous language and figures of speech; by *logic* he is trained in the organization of the intellectual faculties with which he has been endowed; by *arithmetic* he not only is instructed in the mystery of universal order but also gains the key to multitude, magnitude, and proportion; by *geometry* he is inducted into the mathematics of form, the harmony and rhythm of angles, and the philosophy of organization; by *music* he is reminded that the universe is founded upon the laws of celestial harmonics and that harmony and rhythm are all-pervading; by *astronomy* he gains an understanding of the immensities of time and space, of the proper relationship between himself and the universe, and of the awesomeness of that Unknown Power which is driving the countless stars of the firmament through illimitable space. Equipped with the knowledge

---

reason for their rule, that in perfect building the different members must be in exact symmetrical relations to the whole general scheme. Hence, while transmitting to us the proper arrangements for buildings of all kinds, they were particularly careful to do so in the case of temples of the gods, buildings in which merits and faults usually last forever. * * * Therefore, if it is agreed that number was found out from the human fingers, and that there is a symmetrical correspondent between the members separately and the entire form of the body, in accordance with a certain part selected as standard, we can have nothing but respect for those who, in constructing temples of the immortal gods, have so arranged the members of the works that both the separate parts and the whole design may harmonize in their proportions and symmetry." (See *The Ten Books on Architecture*)

By some it is believed that St. Paul was initiated into the Dionysiac Mysteries, for in the tenth verse of the third chapter of First Corinthians he calls himself a "master-builder" or adept: "According to the grace of God which is given into me, as a wise master-builder, I have laid the foundation and another buildeth thereon. " As survivals of the ancient Dionysiac rites, the two diagrams of Cesariano, accompanying this chapter are of incalculable value to the modern mystic architect.

conferred by familiarity with the liberal arts and sciences, the studious Freemason therefore finds himself confronted by few problems with which he cannot cope.

PART II:

The Dionysiac Architects

The most celebrated of the ancient fraternities of artisans was that of the Dionysiac Architects. This organization was composed exclusively of initiates of the Bacchus-Dionysus cult and was peculiarly consecrated to the science of building and the art of decoration. Acclaimed as being the custodians of a secret and sacred knowledge of architectonics, its members were entrusted with the design and erection of public buildings and monuments. The superlative excellence of their handiwork elevated the members of the guild to a position of surpassing dignity; they were regarded as the master craftsmen of the earth. Because of the first dances held in honor of Dionysus, he was considered the founder and patron of the theater, and the Dionysians specialized in the construction of buildings adapted for the presentation of dramatic performances. In the circular or semicircular orchestra they invariably erected an altar to Æschylus, the famous Greek poet, that while appearing in one of his own plays he was suspected by a mob of angry spectators of revealing one of the profound secrets of the Mysteries and was forced to seek refuge at the altar of Dionysus.

So carefully did the Dionysiac Architects safeguard the secrets of their craft that only fragmentary records exist of their esoteric teachings. John A. Weisse thus sums up the meager data available concerning the order:

"They made their appearance certainly not later than 1000 B.C., and appear to have enjoyed particular privileges and immunities. They also possessed secret means of recognition, and were bound together by special ties only known to themselves. The richer of this fraternity were bound to provide for their poorer brethren. They were divided into communities, governed by a Master and Wardens, and called connected houses. They held a grand festival annually, and were held in high esteem. Their ceremonials were regarded as sacred. It has been claimed that Solomon, at the instance of Hiram, King of Tyre, employed them at his temple and palaces. They were also employed at the construction of the Temple of Diana at Ephesus. They had means of intercommunication all over the then known world, and from them, doubtless, sprang the guilds of the Traveling Masons known in the Middle Ages."

The fraternity of the Dionysiac Architects spread throughout all of Asia Minor, even reaching Egypt and India. They established themselves in nearly all the countries bordering on the Mediterranean, and with the rise of the Roman Empire found their way into Central Europe and even into England. The most stately and enduring buildings in Constantinople, Rhodes, Athens, and Rome were erected by these inspired craftsmen. One of the most illustrious of their number was Vitruvius, the great architect, renowned as the author of *De Architectura Libri Decem*. In the various sections of his book Vitruvius gives several hints as to the philosophy underlying the Dionysiac concept of the principle of symmetry applied to the science of architecture, as derived from a consideration of the proportions established by Nature between the parts and members of the human body. The following extract from Vitruvius on the subject of symmetry is representative:

"The design of a temple depends on symmetry, the principles of which must be most carefully observed by the architect. They are due to proportion. Proportion is a correspondence among the measures of the members of an entire work, and of the whole to a certain part selected as standard. From this result the principles of symmetry. Without symmetry and proportion there can be no principles in the design of any temple; that is, if there is no precise relation between its members, as in the case of those of a well-shaped man. For the human body is so designed by nature that the face, from the chin to the top of the forehead and the lowest roots of the hair, is a tenth part of the whole height; the open hand from the wrist to the tip of the middle finger is just the same; the head from the chin to the crown is an eighth, and with the neck and shoulder from the top of the breast to the lowest roots of the hair is a sixth; from the middle of the breast to the summit of the crown is a fourth. If we take the height of the face itself, the distance from the bottom of the chin to the underside of the nostrils [and from that point] to a line between the eyebrows is the same; from there to the lowest roots of the hair is also a third, comprising the forehead. The length of the foot is one sixth of the height of the body; of the forearm, one fourth; and the breadth of the breast is also one fourth. The other members, too, have their own symmetrical proportions, and it was by employing them that the famous painters and sculptors of antiquity attained to great and endless renown."

The edifices raised by the Dionysiac Builders were indeed "sermons in stone." Though unable to comprehend fully the cosmic principles thus embodied in these masterpieces of human ingenuity and industry, even the uninitiated were invariably overwhelmed by the sense of majesty and symmetry resulting from the perfect coordination of pillars, spans, arches, and domes. By variations in the details of size, material, type, arrangement, ornamentation, and color, these inspired builders believed it possible to provoke in the nature of the onlooker certain distinct mental or emotional reactions. Vitruvius, for example, describes the disposition of bronze vases about a room so as to produce certain definite changes in the tone and quality of the human voice. In like manner, each chamber in the Mysteries through which the candidate passed had its own peculiar acoustics. Thus, in one chamber the voice of the priest was amplified until his words caused the very room to vibrate, while in another the voice was diminished and softened to such a degree that it sounded like the distant tinkling of silver bells. Again, in some of the underground passageways the candidate was apparently bereft of the power of speech, for though he shouted at the top of his voice not even a whisper was audible to his ears. After progressing a few feet, however, he would discover that his softest sigh would be reechoed a hundred times.

The supreme ambition of the Dionysiac Architects was the construction of buildings which would create distinct impressions consistent with the purpose for which the structure itself was designed. In common with the Pythagoreans, they believed it possible by combinations of straight lines and curves to induce any desired mental attitude or emotion. They labored, therefore, to the end of producing a building perfectly harmonious with the structure of the universe itself. They may have even believed that an edifice so constructed because it was in no respect at variance with any existing reality would not be subject to dissolution but would endure throughout the span of mortal time. As a logical deduction from their philosophic trend of thought, such a building--en *rapport* with Cosmos--would also have become an oracle. Certain early works on magical philosophy hint that the Ark of the Covenant was oracular in character because of specially prepared chambers in its interior. These by their shape and arrangement were so attuned to the vibrations of the invisible world that they caught and amplified the voices of the ages imprinted upon and eternally existent in the substance of the astral light.

Unskilled in these ancient subtleties of their profession,

modern architects often create architectural absurdities which would cause their creators to blush with shame did they comprehend their actual symbolic import. Thus, phallic emblems are strewn in profusion among the adornments of banks, office buildings, and department stores. Christian churches also may be surmounted with Brahmin or Mohammedan domes or be designed in a style suitable for a Jewish synagogue or a Greek temple to Pluto. These incongruities may be considered trivial in importance by the modern designer, but to the trained psychologist the purpose for which a building was erected is frustrated in large measure by the presence of such architectural discordances. Vitruvius thus defines the principle of propriety as conceived and applied by the Dionysians:

"Propriety is that: perfection of style which comes when a work is authoritatively constructed on approved principles. It arises from prescription from usage, or from nature. From prescription, in the case of hypæthral edifices, open to the sky, in honor of Jupiter Lightning, the Heaven, the Sun, or the Moon: for these are gods whose semblances and manifestations we behold before our very eyes in the sky when it is cloudless and bright. The temples of Minerva, Mars, and Hercules will be Doric, since the virile strength of these gods makes daintiness entirely inappropriate to their houses. In temples to Venus, Flora, Proserpine, Spring-Water, and the Nymphs, the Corinthian order will be found to have peculiar significance, because these are delicate divinities and so its rather slender outlines, its flowers, leaves, and ornamental volutes will lend propriety where it is due. The construction of temples of the Ionic order to Juno, Diana, Father Bacchus, and the other gods of that kind, will be in keeping with the middle position which they hold; for the building of such will be an appropriate combination of the severity of the Doric and the delicacy of the Corinthian."

In describing the societies of Ionian artificers, Joseph Da

Costa declares the Dionysiac rites to have been founded upon the science of astronomy, which by the initiates of this order was correlated to the builder's art. In various documents dealing with the origin of architecture are found hints to the effect that the great buildings erected by these initiated craftsmen were based upon geometrical patterns derived from the constellations. Thus, a temple might be planned according to the constellation of Pegasus or a court of judgment modeled after the constellation of the Scales. The Dionysians evolved a peculiar code by which they were able to communicate with one another in the dark and both the symbols and the terminology of their guild were derived, in the main, from the elements of architecture.

While stigmatized as pagans by reason of their philosophic principles, it is noteworthy that these Dionysiac craftsmen were almost universally employed in the erection of early Christian abbeys and cathedrals, whose stones even to this very day bear distinguishing marks and symbols cut into their surfaces by these illustrious builders. Among the ornate carvings upon the fronts of great churches of the Old World are frequently found representations of compasses, squares, rules, mallets, and clusters of builders' tools skillfully incorporated into mural decorations and even placed in the hands of the effigies of saints and prophets standing in exalted niches. A great mystery was contained in the ancient portals of the Cathedral Of Notre Dame which were destroyed during the French Revolution, for among their carvings were numerous Rosicrucian and Masonic emblems; and according to the records preserved by alchemists who studied their bas-reliefs, the secret processes for metallic transmutation were set forth in their grotesque yet most significant figures.

The checkerboard floor upon which the modern Freemasonic lodge stands is the old tracing board of the Dionysiac

Architects, and while the modern organization is no longer limited to workmen's guilds it still preserves in its symbols the metaphysical doctrines of the ancient society of which it is presumably the outgrowth. The investigator of the origin of Freemasonic symbolism who desires to trace the development of the order through the ages will find a practical suggestion in the following statement of Charles W. Heckethorn:

"But considering that Freemasonry is a tree the roots of which spread through so many soils, it follows that traces thereof must be found in its fruit; that its language and ritual should retain much of the various sects and institutions it has passed through before arriving at their present state, and in Masonry we meet with Indian, Egyptian, Jewish, and Christian ideas, terms therefrom the supreme ambition of their craft and symbols."

The Roman *Collegia* of skilled architects were apparently a subdivision of the greater Ionian body, their principles and organization being practically identical with the older Ionian institution. It has been suspected that the Dionysians also profoundly influenced early Islamic culture, for part of their symbolism found its way into the Mysteries of the dervishes. At one time the Dionysians referred to themselves as Sons of Solomon, and one of the most important of their symbols was the Seal of Solomon--two interlaced triangles. This motif is frequently seen in conspicuous parts of Mohammedan mosques. The Knights Templars--who were suspected of anything and everything--are believed to have contacted these Dionysiac artificers and to have introduced many of their symbols and doctrines into mediæval Europe. But Freemasonry most of all owes to the Dionysiac cult the great mass of its symbols and rituals which are related to the science of architecture. From these ancient and illustrious artisans, it also received the legacy of the unfinished Temple of Civilization-that vast, invisible structure upon which these initiated builders have labored continuously since the inception of their fraternity. This mighty edifice, which has fallen and been rebuilt time after time but whose foundations remain unmoved, is the true Everlasting House of which the temple on the brow of Mount Moriah was but an impermanent symbol.

Aside from the operative aspect of their order, the Dionysiac Architects had a speculative philosophic code. Human society they considered as a rough and untrued ashlar but lately chiseled from the quarry of elemental Nature. This crude block was the true object upon which these skilled craftsmen labored-- polishing it, squaring it, and with the aid of fine carvings transforming it into a miracle of beauty. While mystics released their souls from the bondage of matter by meditation and philosophers found their keenest joy in the profundities of thought, these master workmen achieved liberation from the Wheel of Life and Death by learning to swing their hammers with the same rhythm that moves the swirling forces of Cosmos. They venerated the Deity under the guise of a Great Architect and Master Craftsman who was ever gouging rough ashlars from the fields of space and truing them into universes. The Dionysians affirmed constructiveness to be the supreme expression of the soul, and attuning themselves with the ever-visible constructive natural processes going on around them, believed immortality could be achieved by thus becoming a part of the creative agencies of Nature.

PART III:

Solomon, the Personification of Universal Wisdom

The name Solomon may be divided into three syllables, SOL-OM-ON, symbolizing light, glory, and truth collectively and respectively. The Temple of Solomon is, therefore, first of all "the House of Everlasting Light," its earthly symbol being the temple of stone on the brow of Mount Moriah. According to the Mystery teachings, there are three Temples of Solomon--as there are three Grand Masters, three Witnesses, and three Tabernacles of the Transfiguration. The first temple is the Grand House of the Universe, in the midst of which sits the sun (SOL) upon his golden throne. The twelve signs of the zodiac as Fellow-Craftsmen gather around their shining lord. Three lights--the stellar, the solar, and the lunar--illuminate this Cosmic Temple. Accompanied by his retinue of planets, moons, and asteroids, this Divine King (SOLomon), whose glory no earthly monarch shall ever equal, passes in stately pomp down the avenues of space. Whereas *Hiram* represents the active physical light of the sun, SOLomon signifies its invisible but all-powerful, spiritual and intellectual effulgency.

The second symbolic temple is the human body-the Little House made in the image of the Great Universal House. "Know ye not," asked the Apostle Paul, "that ye are the temple of God, and that the Spirit of God dwelleth in you?" Freemasonry within a temple of stone cannot be other than speculative, but Freemasonry within the living temple of the body is operative. The third symbolic temple is the *Soular* House (rooted in the human soul), an invisible structure, the comprehension of which is a supreme Freemasonic arcanum. The mystery of this intangible edifice is concealed under the allegory of the *Soma Psuchicon,* or Wedding Garment described by St. Paul, the Robes of Glory of the High Priest of Israel, the Yellow Robe of the Buddhist monk, and the Robe of Blue and Gold to which Albert Pike refers in his *Symbolism.* The soul, constructed

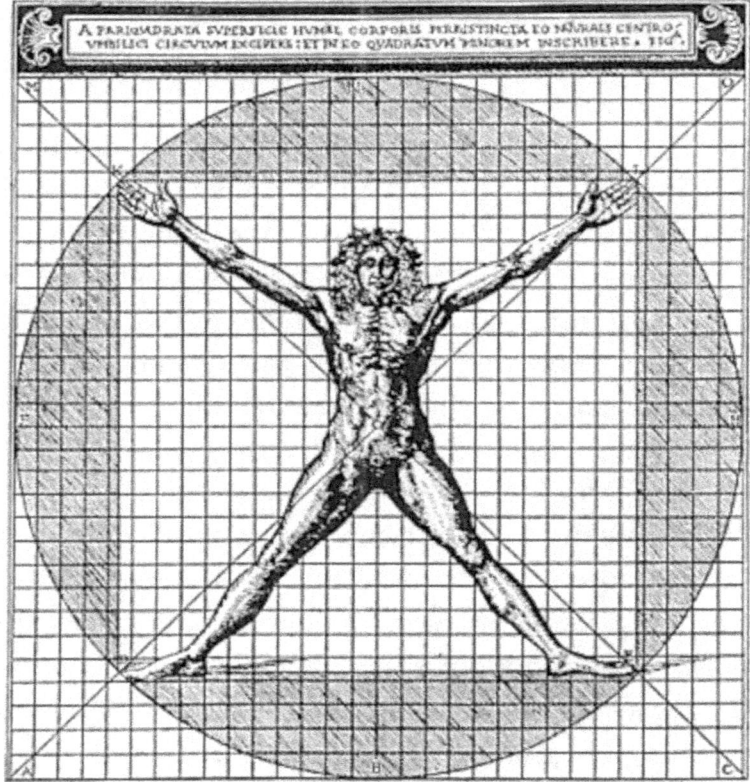

THE MYSTERY OF THE MICROCOSM[2]

---

[2] Redrawn from *Cesariano's Edition of Vitruvius.*

Herein is depicted the mysterious *Word* of Plato which was crucified in space before the foundation of the world. The anonymous author of *The Canon* writes:

"The Logos or soul of the world, according to Plato, the Greek Hermes, and the Christ, according to the Christian Gnostics, are all one and the same as the Hebrew Adam Kadmon, who is the second person of the cabalistic triad. The Cyllenian Hermes, described by Hippolytus, so exactly resembles the lesser from an invisible fiery substance, a flaming golden metal, is cast by the Master Workman, Hiram Abiff, into the mold of clay (the physical body) and is called the Molten Sea. The temple of the human soul is built by three Master Masons personifying Wisdom, Love, and Service, and when constructed according to the Law of Life the spirit of God dwells in the Holy Place thereof. The *Soular* Temple is the true Everlasting House, and he who can *raise* or *cast* it is a Master Mason *indeed!* The best-informed Masonic writers have realized that Solomon's Temple is a representation in miniature of the Universal Temple. Concerning this point, A. E. Waite, in *A New Encyclopædia of Freemasonry,* writes: "It is macrocosmic in character, so that the Temple is a symbol of the universe, a type of manifestation itself."

Solomon, the Spirit of Universal Illumination--mental, spiritual, moral, and physical--is personified in the king of an earthly nation. While a great ruler by that name may have built a temple, he who considers the story solely from its historical angle will never clear away the rubbish that covers the secret vaults. The *rubbish* is interpolated matter in the form of superficial symbols, allegories,

---

man found in Cesariano's edition of Vitruvius, that they may be justifiably considered to be identical."

After relating the figure to Dionysus because of the vine leaves wound in the hair, the same writer concludes: "Here we have clearly and distinctly a curious survival of the cosmic deity of Greece, copied and disfigured by the crude draughtsmen of the Middle Ages, but faithfully preserved, and recognizable to the last." Similar figures are to be found in Agrippa's *De Occulta Philosophia.* Like Cesariano's diagrams, however, the key given for their interpretation is most inadequate. Agrippa declares that, being a type of the lesser world, man contains in himself all numbers, measures, weights, motions, and elements. The secret doctrine of Freemasonry, like that of the Dionysiac Architects, is concerned primarily with the effort to measure or estimate philosophically the parts and proportions of the microcosm, so that by the knowledge derived therefrom the supreme ambition of their craft might be realized--the creation of a perfect man.

and degrees which have no legitimate part in the original Freemasonic Mysteries. Concerning the loss of the true esoteric key to Masonic secrets, Albert Pike writes:

"No one journeys now 'from the high place of Cabaon to the threshing floor of Oman the Yebusite,' nor has seen, 'his Master, clothed in blue and gold;' nor are apprentices and Fellow-crafts any longer paid at their respective Columns; nor is the Master's working tool the Tracing Board, nor does he use in his work 'Chalk, Charcoal, and an Earthen Vessel,' nor does the Apprentice, becoming a Fellow Craft, pass from the square to the compass; for the meanings of these phrases as symbols have long been lost."

According to the ancient Rabbins, Solomon was an initiate of the Mystery schools and the temple which he built was actually a house of initiation containing amass of pagan philosophic and phallic emblems. The pomegranates, the palm-headed columns, the Pillars before the door, the Babylonian cherubim, and the arrangement of the chambers and draperies all indicate the temple to have been patterned after the sanctuaries of Egypt and Atlantis. Isaac Myer, in *The Qabalah,* makes the following observation:

"The pseudo-Clement of Rome, writes: 'God made man male and female. The male is Christ: the female, the Church.' The Qabalists called the Holy Spirit, the mother, and the Church of Israel, the Daughter. Solomon engraved on the walls of his Temple, likenesses of the male and female principles, to adumbrate this mystery; such, it is said, were the figures of the cherubim. This was, however, not in obedience to the words of the Torah. They were symbolical of the Upper, the spiritual, the former or maker, positive or male, and the Lower, the passive, the negative or female, formed or made by the first."

Masonry came to Northern Africa and Asia Minor from the

lost continent of Atlantis, not under its present name but rather under the general designation Sun and Fire Worship. The ancient Mysteries did not cease to exist when Christianity became the world's most powerful religion. Great Pan did not die! Freemasonry is the proof of his survival. The pre-Christian Mysteries simply assumed the symbolism of the new faith, perpetuating through its emblems and allegories the same truths which had been the property of the wise since the beginning of the world. There is no true explanation, therefore, for Christian symbols save that which is concealed within pagan philosophy. Without the mysterious keys carried by the hierophants of the Egyptian, Brahmin, and Persian cults the gates of Wisdom cannot be opened. Consider with reverent spirit, therefore, the sublime allegory of the Temple and its Builders, realizing that beneath its literal interpretation lies hidden a Royal Secret.

According to the Talmudic legends, Solomon understood the mysteries of the Qabalah. He was also an alchemist and a necromancer, being able to control the dæmons, and from them and other inhabitants of the invisible worlds he secured much of his wisdom. In his translation of *Clavicula Salomonis,* or *The Key of Solomon the King,* a work presumably setting forth the magical secrets gathered by Solomon and used by him in the conjuration of spirits and which, according to Frank C. Higgins, contains many sidelights on Masonic initiatory rituals, S. L. MacGregor-Mathers recognizes the probability that King Solomon was a magician in the fullest sense of that word. "I see no reason to doubt," he affirms, "the tradition which assigns the authorship of the 'Key' to King Solomon, for among others Josephus, the Jewish historian, especially mentions the magical works attributed to that monarch; this is confirmed by many Eastern traditions, and his magical skill is frequently mentioned in the Arabian Nights."

Concerning Solomon's supernatural powers, Josephus writes in his *Eighth Book of the Antiquities of the Jews:*

"Now the sagacity and wisdom which God had bestowed on Solomon was so great that he exceeded the ancients, in so much that he was no way inferior to the Egyptians, who are said to have been beyond all men in understanding; God also enabled him to learn that skill which expelled demons, which is a science useful and sanative to him. He composed such incantations also by which distempers are alleviated. And he left behind him the manner of using exorcisms, by which they drive away demons, so that they never return; and this method of cure is of great force unto this day."

The mediæval alchemists were convinced that King Solomon understood the secret processes of Hermes by means of which it was possible to multiply metals. Dr. Bacstrom writes that the *Universal Spirit* (Hiram) assisted King Solomon to build his temple, because Solomon being wise in the wisdom of alchemy knew how to control this incorporeal essence and, setting it to work for him, caused the invisible universe to supply him with vast amounts of gold and silver which most people believed were mined by natural methods.

The mysteries of the Islamic faith are now in the keeping of the dervishes--men who, renouncing worldliness, have withstood the test of a thousand and one days of temptation. Jelal-ud-din, the great Persian Sufic poet and philosopher, is accredited with having founded the Order of Mevlevi, or the "dancing dervishes," whose movements exoterically signify the motions of the celestial bodies and esoterically result in the establishment of a rhythm which stimulates the centers of spiritual consciousness within the dancer's body.

"According to the mystical canon, there are always on earth

a certain number of holy men who are admitted to intimate communion with the Deity. The one who occupies the highest position among his contemporaries is called the 'Axis' (Qutb) or 'Pole' of his time. Subordinate to the Qutb are two holy beings who bear the title of 'The Faithful Ones,' and are assigned places on his right and left respectively. Below these is a quartette of 'Intermediate Ones' (Evtad); and on successively lower planes ate five 'Lights' (Envar), and seven 'Very Good' (Akhyar). The next rank is filled by forty 'Absent Ones' (Rijal-i-ghaib), also termed 'Martyrs' (Shuheda). When an 'Axis' quits this earthly existence, he is succeeded by the 'Faithful One' who has occupied the place at his right hand. For to these holy men, who also bear the collective titles of 'Lords of Souls,' and 'Directors,' is committed a spiritual supremacy over mankind far exceeding the temporal authority of earthly rulers."

The *Axis* is a mysterious individual who, unknown and unsuspected, mingles with mankind and who, according to tradition, has his favorite seat upon the roof of the Caaba. J. P. Brown, in *The Dervishes,* gives a description of these "Master Souls."

PART IV:

Freemasonry's Priceless Heritage

The *sanctum sanctorum* of Freemasonry is ornamented with the gnostic jewels of a thousand ages; its rituals ring with the divinely inspired words of seers and sages. A hundred religious have brought their gifts of wisdom to its altar; arts and sciences unnumbered have contributed to its symbolism. Freemasonry is a world-wide university, teaching the liberal arts and sciences of the soul to all who will hearken to its words. Its chairs are seats of learning and its pillars uphold an arch of universal education. Its trestleboards are inscribed with the eternal verities of all ages and upon those who comprehend its sacred depths has dawned the realization that within the Freemasonic Mysteries lie hidden the long-lost arcana sought by all peoples since the genesis of human reason.

The philosophic power of Freemasonry lies in its symbols-- its priceless heritage from the Mystery schools of antiquity. In a letter to Robert Freke Gould, Albert Pike writes:

"It began to shape itself to my intellectual vision into something more imposing and majestic, solemnly mysterious and grand. It seemed to me like the Pyramids in their loneliness, in whose yet undiscovered chambers may be hidden, for the enlightenment of coming generations, the sacred books of the Egyptians, so long lost to the world; like the Sphynx half buried in the desert. In its symbolism, which and its spirit of brotherhood are its essence, Freemasonry is more ancient than any of the world's living religions. It has the symbols and doctrines which, older than himself, Zarathustra inculcated; and ii seemed to me a spectacle sublime, yet pitiful--the ancient Faith of our ancestors holding out to the world its symbols once so eloquent, and mutely and in vain asking for an interpreter. And so I came at last to see that the true greatness and majesty of Freemasonry consist in its proprietorship of these and its other symbols; and that its symbolism is its soul."

Though the temples of Thebes and Karnak be now but majestic heaps of broken and time-battered stone, the spirit: of Egyptian philosophy still marches triumphant through the centuries. Though the rock-hewn sanctuaries of the ancient Brahmins be now deserted and their carvings crumbled into dust, still the wisdom of the Vedas endures. Though the oracles be silenced and the House of the Mysteries be now but rows of ghostly columns, still shines the spiritual glory of Hellas with luster undiminished. Though Zoroaster, Hermes, Pythagoras, Plato, and Aristotle are now but dim memories in a world once rocked by the transcendency of their intellectual genius, still in the mystic temple of Freemasonry these god- men live again in their words and symbols; and the candidate, passing through the initiations, feels himself face to face with these illumined hierophants of days long past.

Other Books in this Series and Related Titles

Nature Spirits and Elementals by Louise Off (978-1-63118-605-9)

Swedenborg Bifrons by H P Blavatsky (978-1-63118-604-2)

Practical Use of Psychic Powers by C W Leadbeater (978-1-63118-603-5)

Using White & Black Magic by C W Leadbeater (978-1-63118-602-8)

Jesus, the Last Great Initiate by Edouard Schure (978-1-63118-599-1)

Mysterious Wonders of Antiquity by Manly P Hall (978-1-63118-598-4)

Ancient Mysteries and Secret Societies by Manly P Hall (978–1–63118–597–7)

The Zodiac and Its Signs by Manly P Hall (978–1–63118–596–0)

Life and Teachings of Hermes Trismegistus by Manly P Hall (978–1–63118–595–3)

The Secrets of Doctor Taverner by Dion Fortune (978–1–63118–594–6)

Vegetarianism, Theosophy & Occultism by Leadbeater &c (978–1–63118–593–9)

Applied Theosophy by Henry S Olcott (978–1–63118–592–2)

Higher Consciousness by C W Leadbeater (978–1–63118–591–5)

Theories About Reincarnation and Spirits by H P Blavatsky (978–1–63118–590–8)

The Use and Power of Thought by C W Leadbeater (978–1–63118–589–2)

Commentary on the Pymander by G R S Mead (978–1–63118–588–5)

Hypnotism and Mesmerism by Annie Besant (978–1–63118–587–8)

Spirits of Various Kinds by Helena P Blavatsky (978–1–63118–586–1)

The Hidden Language of Symbolism by Annie Besant (978–1–63118–585–4)

Eastern Magic & Western Spiritualism by Henry S Olcott (978–1–63118–584–7)

Spiritual Progress and Practical Occultism by H P Blavatsky (978–1–63118–583–0)

Audio versions are also available on Audible, Amazon and Apple

Other Books in this Series and Related Titles

Memory and Consciousness by Besant & Blavatsky (978–1–63118–582–3)

The Origin of Evil by Helena P Blavatsky (978–1–63118–581–6)

The Camp of Philosophy: Studies in Alchemy by Bloomfield (978–1–63118–580–9)

The Testaments of the Twelve Patriarchs (978–1–63118–579–3)

Occult or Exact Science? by Helena P Blavatsky (978–1–63118–578–6)

Occultism, Semi-Occultism & Pseudo Occultism by A Besant (978–1–63118–577–9)

The Fourth-Gospel and Synoptical Problem by G R S Mead (978–1–63118–576–2)

On the Bhagavad-Gita by T Subba Row &c (978–1–63118–575–5)

What Theosophy Does for Us by C W Leadbeater (978–1–63118–574–8)

Spiritual Life for Man by Annie Besant (978–1–63118–573–1)

The Mysteries by Annie Besant (978–1–63118–572–4)

Fundamental Ideas of Theosophy by Bhagwan Das (978–1–63118–571–7)

Dreams: What They Are and How They Are Caused (978–1–63118–570–0)

Communication Between Different Worlds by Annie Besant (978–1–63118–569–4)

Animism, Magic and the Omnipotence of Thought by S Freud (978–1–63118–568–7)

Buddhism by F Otto Schrader (978–1–63118–567–0)

Death by W W Westcott (978–1–63118–566–3)

The Religion of Theosophy by Bhagwan Das (978–1–63118–565–6)

The Spirit of Zoroastrianism by Henry S Olcott (978–1–63118–564–9)

The Brotherhood of Religions by Annie Besant (978–1–63118–563–2)

Fourth Book of Maccabees by Josephus (978-1-63118-562-5)

Audio versions are also available on Audible, Amazon and Apple

www.ingramcontent.com/pod-product-compliance
Lightning Source LLC
LaVergne TN
LVHW041503070426
835507LV00009B/788